Inland Sea

Also by Brenda Saunders
Firestick (Mayn Press, 2011)
Looking for Bullen Bullen (Hybrid Press, 2012)
the sound of red (Ginninderra Press, 2013)

Brenda Saunders

Inland Sea

Acknowledgements

Many poems in this collection have been published in poetry journals both in print and online, including *Australian Poetry Journal, Mascara Literary Review, Cordite, Overland, Plumwood Mountain, Quadrant, Southerly, Stylus Lit, Westerly* and *VerityLa*. Other poems have also appeared in newspapers, online sites and edited anthologies including *Best Australian Prose Poetry 2020* and *Best Australian Science Writing 2020*.

Poems have also been awarded prizes in national competitions including 'Quondongs', the 2018 Oodgeroo Noonuccal Prize (Queensland Poetry), 'Scarred Landscape', the 2018 Joanne Burns Award (Spineless Wonders) and 'Windorah', the 2016 Banjo Patterson Bush Poetry Prize. ''Spinifex rings' (Microcosmos) was longlisted for the 2014 Vice-Chancellor's International Poetry Prize, Canberra University.

Looking for Bullen Bullen was awarded the 2014 Scanlon Book Prize (Australian Poetry Inc) and the 2013 Poetry Book Prize (Woollahra Literary Festival). Several of these poems were translated into French for publication by the University of Cergy-Paris, France.

Thanks to the Varuna International Writers' House for their generosity. The Mick Dark Environmental Fellowship and the First Nations Fellowship were of great assistance in the production of this book. Special thanks to Ginninderra Press for their commitment to Australian poetry and to my colleagues from Round Table Poets and Young Street Poets for their ongoing criticism and support.

Inland Sea
ISBN 978 1 76109 144 5
Copyright © Brenda Saunders 2021
Cover image: Brenda Saunders, *Red Centre*, mixed media on paper

First published 2021 by
GINNINDERRA PRESS
PO Box 3461 Port Adelaide 5015
www.ginninderrapress.com.au

Contents

dead centre — 7
    Echidna Chasm — 9
    Spinifex rings — 10
    inland sea — 12
    Dead Centre — 14
    Scarred Landscape — 16
    Red Centre — 17
    Storm over the Tanami — 18
    Walmadany — 19
    Kumerang — 21
    Poor fella Country — 23
    Spirit of Country — 24
    Piccaninny Gorge — 26
    Windorah — 28
    Feral — 30

dry run — 31
    Native Title — 33
    Silverton — 34
    Walking on water — 35
    yellow vest — 36
    dry run — 37
    canopy — 38
    Lightning strike — 39
    Understorey — 41
    Rich pickings — 43
    dawn chorus — 44
    calling — 45
    captive — 46
    whiplash — 47
    bird brain — 48

right season   49

    Quandongs, La Pa   51
    Bush Tucker Tour   52
    Mingkulpa   53
    Smoke   54
    Firestick Farming   55
    Black boys   56
    Wild Honey Tour   57
    Wirilda   58
    Mulga stories   59
    Lillipilli   61
    Larrkardiy   62

dark harvest   63

    People of the River: Derrubban   65
    People of the River: Backwater   66
    Figures in a landscape   67
    Monument   69
    At the Falls Bundanoon I   70
    At the Falls Bundanoon II   71
    Bennelong   72
    Cullen Bullen   73
    Lady Mungo   75
    Nukkan ya, Ruby: 'See you, Ruby'   76
    Jandamarra   77
    Boab Tree, Derby   78
    Jaga Jaga   79
    Earth hour   80
    Singing the land   81

Notes   82

dead centre

Echidna Chasm

Only her Dreaming remains
her Gidgi-Djaru name lost   blown away
with the blight of conquest
on Purnululu

She leads us through a narrow cleft
sheer walls scraped clean
with her spiny back   a gorge   red hot
bounces from white light to shadow
the sky a blue slit above

Rounded sockets mark her journey
the ball of a heel   a trail left behind
as she rushes through mud   shaping
Bungle Bungle Country

Year after year she lays her giant eggs
in the chamber   bone white
glazed by time   tossed free
with the rush of water
by the unstoppable river in flood

Mystery lingers   silent echoes
fill this tight ravine   great marbles
spilling at the mouth
onto a plain bright with sunshine.

Spinifex rings

Grey green rings spread across the sand
hold water underground. In spiky tufts
a tiny world exists, silent and unseen

These creatures hide in rasping folds
of hummock grass, hunt with night vision
for invisible gnats breeding in shadow

caught off guard by a cloudy moon

Corellas fly low over lignum brush, swing
and dip on a spinifex stalk. Sharp eyes
spy a beetle or moth in their path

Marsupial mice build a storehouse for seeds
in burrows underground, alerted at dusk
by insects humming across the desert floor

Rusty coats trick their unsuspecting prey

A barking spider sits in a hole no larger
than a camera lens, stretches a fine mesh
around her nest, waits patiently for a tremor

on the line. She passes long years measured
in our slow time, sends her spiderlings
floating on gossamer. Caught by the wind

they are easy game for a little grassbird
flitting about, hanging her cup-like nest high
on a stem of cumbungi, away from spiky lizards

Criss-crossing the ring, termites ease
their way through a web of tunnels, feed
on dead roots, grass seeds left in their path

follow patterns passed down in memory

A pygmy goanna leaves ornate tracks
as he swings along, senses a line of bull ants
in their cone-shaped nest. They fix a door

from curling mulga leaves, ward off
big rains coming down from the north
rest tight in the nest until the storm passes

Each year a stick-nest rat explores her circle
of dens, repairs each coverlet of twigs
A mound of pebbles collects rare dewdrops

seals the home from predators

A tawny dunnart sits, waiting to pounce
Large eyes gleam as she snaps at a spider
takes over his empty hole, sleeps through heat

days of waiting for rain and the time to breed

Measured by a finger length, these creatures
hold on through changing seasons, their span
of life slowed down to desert time. Stillness

A grassy ring holding their world in place.

inland sea

clay pans shrink to pools
in the trail of a wet season
hold a micro cosmos
teeming with life

red-finned gobies
flash a miniature flame
though tiny succulents

carnivores varied as coral
wave vivid flowers
trick insects
to their water garden

under a shrinking puddle
snails with no shell
dig in for the long hot spell

termite mounds signpost
a desert soak after rain
green shoots on cumbungi
a magic lure for butterflies

banded finches, zit, flit
in button grass, bring sound
and action to the silent pond

dragonflies, water striders
hover, buzz the fetid air
with new life as the system
gives way to wild extremes

low rainfall, high winds
bare earth eroding
every gully under the sun

stored a million years ago
water from the inland sea
flows in ancient channels
underground

rises in sacred 'gnammas'
hidden rock mounds
keeping the desert alive

farmers running cattle
bore into the basin
compete with the micro life
on a land with no water

wild creatures struggle
to hold on, lose the fight
through every failing season

Dead Centre

notes from *Expedition to Central Australia*, Charles Sturt, 1844–46

We stood as it were in the centre of a dark and gloomy sea of scrub without a break in its monotonous surface... I could not but think that we could not be very far from the outskirts of an inland sea, it so precisely resembled a low and barren sea coast...

– warnings came by 'mulga wire', a mob of *guuwiyn* with strange animals dragging a big canoe through sand. The great rivers were dry, so we showed them right place to dig on Mithaka land, find water –

On our journey we were all suffering from scurvy; and the heat was intense... We noted a new species, heaps of which had been gathered by the natives for seed...

– they crossed into Kullila Country uninvited, wild with the 'sickness'. We yelled, 'migkan dura', gave them roasted wattle seeds, bush medicine, but they did not share our tribal ways –

I did regret that the progress of civilized man in to an uncivilized region would inevitably bring misfortune to those living here the original inhabitants...but on our way we always made allowances for the timidity and prejudices of the natives...

– we thought them Spirit Men, roaming in 'dry time'. What did they want on Putti Putti land? We let them pass, watched them push on through stone country where no man would walk –

We were gradually and steadily working our way into the interior. A chill fear took hold of me...our world became little more than a rolling shingly plain...at the Dead Heart...

A blood red sea, the gibber lay before us, weirdly, horribly solemn: a sea over which the ghosts of ships and men might revel for eternity...

hope
a promised sea
shimmers the horizon

a wooden boat
rides waves
of disbelief

endeavour
tests mortality
dead centre

dominion
drives every footstep
of the valiant

Scarred Landscape

The plane flies low over a curve of red ochre country. Landforms scatter. A waterhole stretches the horizon. Trees flash by in a line of grey. My window lifts to frame the sky, dips to saltpans turning blue after rain. The perspective tilts, pulls a mine into focus. Moving like ants, giant loaders dredge the inside out of the iron ore plain. Tailings bury a world of stillness, reshape a landscape of tussock grass, spinifex rings holding the desert in place. At a slow angle man-made hills rise to meet us. Blow raw dust into a heaving sky.

Red Centre

The Caterpillar Man, Yeperenye, moves across the land,
his spiky backbone folds, softens in Namatjira sunlight.
He goes under the Sheraton, drinks the Todd River dry.

At the airport white heat bounces off galvanized tin.
Bulldozers crumble the last hump of the Caterpillar Man
as the CIA builds a runway, seals the road to Pine Gap.

Planes bump in to Yulara on the hour. Coach convoys
buzz and brim, hit the bitumen on Lasseter's highway,
tracking the journey of Kunija, the Spirit Snake

in an epic world where everything is possible.

*

Mparntwe springs lie reflex blue in a rim of rock.
From the camp nearby women shuffle red earth,
dance a mulga ant story. Amaze the drop-in tourists.

Clothes flap and flag as they climb the Rock. Some fall,
some die. Boots wear down tracks of the Mala wallaby.
Visitors scream as they conquer the world Down Under,

look up, wave to a sky writer trailing Joy Rides Are Us.

Some take souvenirs, send them back, complaining
of bad luck. The Mala woman's grief weighs down stones
in their pockets. She sighs, finds her tchurunga stolen,

stored in a city museum, for safety and posterity.

Storm over the Tanami

In the Big Wet, monsoon clouds
blow in from the Arafura, stretch
a line of black on the horizon
Across the rusty plain a willi willi
circles a fury of sand, blows
raw dust into a heaving sky
Spinifex, tussock grass hold
the land in place, hide a world
of stillness on this stony ground
Small creatures thrive, survive
wild seasons, keep the desert alive.

Walmadany

Footsteps of giant creatures cross the ancient mud
A thousand paw prints caught in pitted sandstone
run along the shore, fill as rock pools at high tide

The Goolarabaroo sing the trail of a Marrala man
A great emu races by, shedding feathers from his tail
Leaves fern-like patterns pressed into rock

Their lives are linked to greater cycles, moving stars
Seven Sisters Dreaming spans the sky to Uluru
moves further east as far as 'sunrise country'

Today the white men have come to take the inside
out of our country. Search in places far deeper
than the Snake Man shaping the land long ago

Woodside have found gas under the ocean
offer leases, promise wealth to the shrinking tribes
to young men drifting to towns down south

The people make a stand on different grounds
one group against the other. Some welcome change
new ideas, share the white man's dreams

Others know the land is not theirs to give. Hold to
the natural law. Traditional men fear the talk
of pipelines, jetties, a gas hub along the bay

For centuries they walk the Lurrujarri Dreaming
sing the songlines along the coastal plain. Follow
the seasons on 'the land where the sun goes down'

Back from the dunes, shell middens lie bleached
and massed. Spearheads, grinding tools left
unguarded, testify to years of Ceremony

They watch for whales calving off the cliff
trap dugongs in channels on the turquoise reef
feasting on turtle eggs laid under warm sand

Their footsteps tread lightly on Country. Swept
by wind and tide they leave no sign of possession
their imprint easily lost to the weight of change

A swinging ball is no match for memories stored
in sand, sacred stories stretching to Walmadany
Their hero spirit looks down, guards the Point

his ochre cliffs hold fire from a falling sun. Belief
lies deeper than the promise of riches. Invisible gas
captured offshore, flowing under a darkening sea.

Kumerang

'I was told, you can't do them things any more. Too much white government...you know. So I think if I didn't speak out now, we would have lost it all.' – Doreen Kartinyeri

She sits with the other Yarraldi women
under the shadow of the fatal bridge, speaks
of Secret Women's Business. 'Knowledge'
she could never share with clansmen
or white lawyers seeking confirmation

So they sought guidance from the Elders upriver,
advice on Ngarrendjeri heritage. Sacred lore
along the Coorong. Men who knew nothing
of the Women's secret places on the island

Born on a mission far from the river, she knows
the dangers of losing language, the clans
set apart. Keeps the stories passed down from
her aunties, speaks of Creation Time, places
of birth, death, shaping Women's Dreaming

From the sky, the channels cup the island
map a great womb washed clean at high tide
Fresh water once ran full and deep here
surged through the canal to meet the sea

The women speak of loss, the long fight to save
the island from development. 'The Bridge'
now a link for cars, four-wheel drives, roads
to a new marina, their sacred birthing places
buried under parks and concrete slabs

Time to save the great river winding through
dry country upstream, the flow controlled
by dams, towns along the river's edge. Farmers
building pipelines, pumps to slake a thirsty land

Downstream the estuary lies back, thirsty
at low tide. In summer, the fresh stream runs
to a trickle. Ferries sit at the jetty, powerboats
cruisers, complain of sandy channels, a bridge
built too low for tall yachts to pass through

The island speaks of failed tourist ventures
Holiday flats, a man-made marina still empty
Fish no longer swim in the still, saline estuary
ancient feeding sites for the Sacred Pelican

The old Coorong has the last say to folly. Men
with prospects ignore the warning, as the sea
goes on filling the mouth with sand. Year-long
dredges battle against time and stupidity
to forge a water course flowing out to sea

The women ignore the arc spanning above
hold fast their memories of a time before
'progress' destroyed the estuary for everyone
reshaped their Yarraldi culture forever.

Poor fella Country

Up north a patchwork map divides the land
in leases, ready for a pipeline to pump the gas
offshore. Miners on the move, trace cracks

shifting underground, pierce bedrock to the core
searching for a liquid fire brighter than oil
Build pipelines to store the gas offshore, ship

new power to a world hungry for more

Pushed and shoved, the landscape resettles
Mountains razed, line up as piles of shale
– loose molehills spin dust on the wind

In the Kimberley, machines carve a range
into squared hills, the ore sliced and trucked
to ports down south. Up in the Bight, Xstrata

move a river sideways to mine the stony bed

At Alice Old Men 'Dream-up' the Sacred Caterpillar
as machines cut a road through his golden back
Roads drawn on a gouged-out plain go nowhere

once the last seam has failed and the magic spent

Scattered clans can no longer care for Country
Without Language, the Elders have no power
over young ones living the white man's dream.

I see sorrow in our people sitting on Country
Wasted in spirit, they suffer, hold a sickness
inside, as mining grinds their stories away.

Buried under scabby ground, danger lies out
of sight. An unseen cloud on future horizons.

Spirit of Country

1.

Warm air in a corner of sky
showers a rainbow
I fly low
    over wooded plains

see patterns
in familiar changes
right time   right season
    read from the sky

Firestick farming   after rain
bush smoulders
smoke drifts a scent of wattle
    seed pods open

Hunters ring a trap
spear wallabies   snakes
escaping heat and fear

I move from to earth to sky
'sing' sacred places
    future harvests

hover   high up
    an eagle's-eye view

warn of darkening currents
new sounds   strangers
    riding onto Country

2.

Between sun and earth
    I circle   watch
      over dying land

Dust hangs a brown haze
on dirt roads   raw stubble
      empty paddocks

beasts fall where they stand

A slow dam flickers white light
on trees
a last ditch waiting

Around my ears insects hum
a loop   stiffened air
dictates the bleakness from here

Caught at the margins of day
      and night
I dip and soar
the black shield arcing above me
'dream up' thunder
    lightning   rainbows

I may never come down   stay
    hooked to clouds
channelling rain songs

sense the wash   the smell of rain
on familiar rivers and creeks

Piccaninny Gorge

'…that's where the spirit is…that's where the Dreaming is.' – Patrick Mung Mung

He paints his Ngarranggarni Dreaming
in ochres from his fathers' Country
Flattens, folds the red-brown hills, loops
a creek-line with a row of white dots.

Each local tribe claims to hold
the true Creation Story, keeps
secret the lore over Bungle Bungle.
There are no names, no guide to
lead us on Gidgi and Djaru Country
Piccaninny a name for 'baby'
found in white men's Dreaming.

Time creeps here, holds secrets
inside these banded walls, the path
forever open to mystery. There is
no Womens' Dreaming to follow
lead us down this dry canal
smoothed each year by a creek
forging through in flood.

I imagine generations of women
walking this sandy bed after rain
has filled the bathing pools
Rock holes cleansed, rounded
by wind and water. Limestone
slaked blue by ancient coral reefs
raised from an inland sea.

Our voices echo, ring a great chasm
open to the sky. Blood-red walls close in.
Womb-like they circle
a pond shining lapiz blue. A miracle
shields this space from change
the spring, a birthing place perhaps
cradling forever the silent water.

Windorah

Each year big rains leave the Diamantina
in flood. The river spreads in channels
runs in fast streams to lakes down south

Drifts of bark and twigs catch in the fork
of trees like forgotten nests of the cockatoo
Lines of mud mark the slurry rushing through

Tiny micro-life survives in soil washed down
with the spill. Drying in silt it lifts off, flies
on the wind in a red-dust storm. Crustaceans

survive the dry season buried under sand
Frogs too lie under silt for years, waiting
for the floods to take them into deeper water

*

The wet season ends once more in a heat haze
A smell of yellow hangs on the air. Insects
search for honey among flowering gidgee

keep up a steady burr intoxicated by nectar
Little corellas swing and dip on Spinifex stalks
waiting for a spider to come their way

A tiny planigale returns home to a clay-pan
cracking in the sun, a baby secure in the pouch
She disturbs gnats swarming in moist shadows

sends them flitting about, their span of a life
shorter than a day. An easy prey to stillness
quick tongues, sharp eyes in the tussock grass.

*

Saltbush runs wild on the Mallee plain
Close to the road heading west, trees thrive
from run-off after rain. Bright honeyeaters

no bigger than a leaf shimmer and dash
hang upside down, unseen among the dazzle
of cherries ripening on a quandong tree

A pygmy glider hovers over flowering scrub
steers her way with a feathery tail, to pluck
the sap of mulga blossoms. Tiny as a mouse

she builds her handball nest in tree trunks
or takes a ready-made instead, holds silent
as night hunters raid her world of shadows.

Feral

He waits for the moon
circles new terrain
survives the wilderness
a moving shadow unchallenged
by vigilantes, fellow travellers
They fear his speed and fury
the swipe of a giant claw
bred from some domestic pet
let go as the family moved on

The desert holds its breath
stunned by the scent
of a night prowler circling
the tussock grass, hunting
his world to extinction.

dry run

Native Title

The currawongs have come to breed
feed on flowering gums in our park
Each year they strut about, stand firm
against invaders crossing their path
teach their young the songs to hold
old nesting sites, reclaim land rights
over territory, a square of grass
framed by cars and bitumen.

Silverton

Solitary, the bird reigns unchallenged
         in this quiet 'ghost town'
holds his vantage point on phone lines
             going nowhere
now the people have moved on

The sacred kingfisher looks down, waits
        for movement on rusting roofs
ignores visitors stirring the dust
to read signs on corrugated shopfronts
             'Saddles', 'Kerosene'
the General Store boarded up for decades

His chuckling 'ch-rr-k' fills the stony citadels
         rises to the church on the hill
the bank once a hub for the silver trade
a courthouse built to serve diggers' justice

Wild days on the moving frontier, financed
         by men rich with success
Long years of prosperity, promises made
      before the mines ran out

Disturbed he swoops, plumage flashing
         satin blue to white
Colours of peace seem fitting for a bird
          that senses the silence
Freedom to fly without fear or threat
        over his treeless domain.

Walking on water

We find the jacanda on an ornamental pond
behind the motel. Lying side-on, in perfect stillness
she appears to enjoy her sunbath. So aptly named
the Christ-bird, this lotus-hopper wakes, steps
quickly from pad to pad on long spreading toes.
Our voices bring a new threat to her sanctuary.
Fear drains the colour from her bright comb.
With aquatic finesse, she turns makes a sudden run,
dives below her floating world. Holding
her snorkel-beak high above the surface she waits,
sensing danger. At the deepwater nest
she scoops up her eggs, tucks them one by one
under her wing. Finds a new hiding place
on the far side, away from prying eyes.

yellow vest

alpha male
struts about
alert to the thud
of footsteps
on the path

small as a finger
the robin
bars our way

full-throated anger
cracks the air
with lungs no bigger
than a pea

supporters chirp
in surround sound
their nests safe
in the fuzz
of wattle

dry run

tall grasses crowd the ditch
last remnant
of a shifting creek

budgerigars flash yellow
a thousand wings lift
a scree scree to the sky

on the turn a green dazzle
swarms in formation
sinks in dusty reeds

at sunset insects hum
the marshy pond, swarm
a yellow fuzz in mimosa

crimson chats flame
in spiky reeds. Afraid
of stillness they flit, whirr

too fast for our eyes to catch
their life slowed down
to endless days in cumbungi

down a sloping bank
a hundred ink blots totter
native hens on red pins

smudge into shadow
slow as a river in drought
they sip one by one

flee at the call of a kite
cruising overhead

canopy

a warbler's song line
carries the sound of a leaf
falling from sunlight

high in the canopy
his bell call rises
ripples the forest awake

a fig parrot flashes red
to green, screams delight
in a bush cherry tree

a spray in one claw
he nibbles, tears
calls 'caw caw' to the sky

in this throwaway world
fruit drops delight a beetle
working the leaf litter

an ant balances a seed
staggers under a load
too big for his back

drags it to the nest
with mandibles
stronger than wire

Lightning strike

After long years of drought the forest
is tinder dry. Grey gums wait for rain
shed their winter bark, drop leaves

to the floor below. Their oily scent
fuels the lightning, sends flames
running to a line of distant hills.

Black stumps stand as giant stakes
driven into a land deserted, now
the fire has passed. Boulders, outcrops

lie exposed on a hillside once screened
with wattle, scrub heavy with nectar.

A single koala runs from hot ashes.
His tarred coat still smoulders
with heat after the trunks have cooled.

Confused he has no defence against
the fury sweeping his tree-top sanctuary

Half-blind he sniffs the smoke haze
finds escape on a line of parched clay
his world no longer defined by canopy.

The spinebill returns to her territory
softened by ash. Built-in sonar
guides her back to her old nesting tree.

With curved bill she pecks at grubs
escaping the sapwood boiling inside.

Tipped with black, her rusty feathers
merge with wounds in the bark
protect her from a whistling kite

eyeing the wasted ground for fresh kill

– snakes in shrinking mud holes
along the banks of a blackened creek.

Understorey

The wood moth lies weightless now
her swollen body free of progeny
A brief life complete after days spent
storing eggs nearby.

Nobody is sure where they live
and grow, waiting for Spring.

She never sees her tiny caterpillars
drifting on threads of silk, blown
by wind and chance in new directions.

Climbing the gum, they tunnel a way
to the juicy sap inside, disguise the nest
with a plug spun from dusky silk.
Trick birds looking for an easy meal.

Aware of these invasions the tree repairs
these itchy intrusions, sends pheromones
into the air signalling danger, as grubs
invade en masse, ring-barking the trunk

hold on as it crashes to the forest floor.

*

Nothing is lost in the sclerophyll.

Deep in the under-storey, everything
is ripe for exploitation. Unobserved
tiny creatures thrive in the half light.

A beetle's long antennae search
the valley floor for fallen eucalypts
finds bark soft enough for her larvae
to burrow, digest the dying tree

prepare their next transformation.

Litter bugs creep at ground level.
Strong and slow, sturdy backs tunnel
musty leaves, funnel everything tossed
by a possum or passing glider.

Soil breathes as they turn over waste
work to keep their silent world alive.

And so it goes as generations of bugs
prepare the earth for new growth.
Send great gums soaring to the canopy.

Rich pickings

Satin bowerbird

Lured by his riffling song
she looks for the violet eye
ignores the scattered bowers
built by young admirers
Accepts the virile male
arching satin wings, his dance
a quiver of reflex blue
In this secret lover's den
he lays out trinkets
of sapphire glass, gold
and silver rings to seal
their wedding tryst
Gaudy offerings spread
with artistry and guile.

Pilot bird

He works alone in filtered light
raking the valley for fallen seeds
Wrongly named, he has no need
to fly high above the canopy
no time to guide the bowerbird
trailing in his wake. Plain
as a twig, this wily bird has
no violet eye, no virile dance
to lead her on and yet she follows
values his darting gait, his speed
and expertise. Profits from
his keen eye for minutiae
rich pickings in the understorey.

dawn chorus

wind gusts loop from branch to branch
shake rain high in the canopy

a quickened fugue wakes the forest
to sound and movement

the rifle bird plays his rasping cello
flashes blue-black in leaves

a warbler's tiny lungs lift his song
above a parrot's staccato warnings

honey eaters pipe in shrill allegretto
a bell minor rings the morning in

pitch perfect, the butcher bird shapes
a riff, startles the air with personality

high or low his greeting finds a space
above the chorale

in the seeming cacophony, pure notes
hang in air, fall down the scale

each bird calls across his sonic arc
holds his song in place

listens for the welcome echo, calling
across the bright abyss

calling

on warm nights I hear the low note
of the koel   on and on he holds
his lonely song   returning each year
to the same tree   to wait   listen
for a mate to call him back

or was that you on the phone
the ringtone echoing
down the empty hall
stirs anxious dreams   of waiting

captive

all day the scrub wren
drills an ache
inside my head
chirps a single note
in ceaseless repetition

wings pressed tight
her heartbeat pulses
confuses sounds
messages
from the world outside

at night she twitters
behind my ear
flutters down tunnels
drumming
against sleep

tips my balance
in dizzying dreams
of soaring

whiplash

a whipbird moves
an elusive flicker
in shadowy ferns
tiny lungs slide
in crescendo
explode in notes
loud with a fury
far beyond his size

a whistle crack
tears the silence
ricochets on the hill
resounds far off

impressed
by his lash
a lone female
submits
her faint
two-note
reply

bird brain

narcissus

alert to danger
a lorikeet has no time
for self-reflection
as he dips to drink
rainbow colours
ring the mirrored pool

    *

lovebird

captive
he kisses
chips
at his lover
trapped
in the cold glint
of mercury

    *

pigeons

always fly home
no matter how many holes
we put them in

right season

Quandongs, La Pa

We go out with the Aunties
to look for quandongs
growing in run-off lines
close to the bitumen
Select bright bush cherries
ready to drop
– a bite too bitter still
for my sweet tooth

The old women
laugh as they sort
pat hot-pink fruit laced
with wild honey

teach us bush tucker way

Each ball rolled on the tongue
sends a sudden shock
to the back of my throat
a sweet-sour hit
– an aftertaste
perfumed
with blossom.

Bush Tucker Tour

We take a well-worn track out to a stand
of desert witjuri, watch
the women dig deep, hack at the treasure
curled safely among the roots
They offer a native snack, a bush challenge
to visitors from the city
– a creamy morsel wriggling on a stick
soft and nutty in the mouth or
a roasted puffball, the comforting hint
of chicken held on the tongue

*

Grandmas with dillybag and stick
once sustained whole families
– the yield from a single tree
an easy meal to fill a hunter's belly

We smell the familiar scent of wattle
as they smoke tnyeme brush
sip a healing tea, bitter as any bush medicine
Children find us a hidden treat
Honeydew, a native sweet to lick
from the underside of leaves.

Mingkulpa

Just out of Alice, we pick up the heady scent
of bush tobacco, go along with the Aunties
to a lush green spread, ripe for plucking
We stuff sticky plants in plastic bags, head back
to town for a sit-down chat, wait 'til the leaves
dry out, curl darker in the sun. Young women

crush the find between grinding stones, add
a pinch of tjulpa from a bloodwood fire, shape
a powdered 'quid' to pop under the tongue
As heat lifts in a slow burn, the women smile
sigh, the mood relaxed as they touch their heads
as if to say 'feelin' good, all worries gone away'

This ancient salve once held great power. Prized
for its potency as a valued barter with the clans
and tribesmen passing through Country
Homeland women keep tradition strong, share
their stock 'old way' with family and friends
Send peace offerings in the mail, to communities

living 'white way'. Precious parcels as a remedy
for sadness and fatigue guaranteed above any
the new fashion for 'roll your own' nicotine
or favourites cigarettes. Marlboro in fancy packs
and Winfield Blue, easily bought at the store
Know the danger from this 'no-good smoke'

as a new sickness spreads in families. Rekindle
belief in the power of mingkulpa, a soothing balm
to heal the body, clear spirit, heart and mind.

Smoke

Smoke always burns the strongest memories.
Wherever we go, we carry with us the smell
of scorched mallee, wattle and river gum.
It lives in our clothes, in layers of skin. Our hair
is still tinged with the scent. Whenever we hear
the crackle, sense the burn, we are back
on the plain, watching a fume of perfumed sap
as mallee roots break open, hold fire long
after the danger has passed. Wattles stand
together, survive the passing fury, leave a hint
of wild honey in the haze. Red gums smoulder
inside, send eucalyptus floating on water. Roots
search below the slow drift of a dying river.

Firestick Farming

If we could go back two hundred years
we would sit here, follow the stars for signs
for right time. Read patterns on the land
Know the right season for burning Country
After heavy dew, we would join farmers
lighting patchwork rings, set fire to bracken
emu grass, leave trees and scrub smouldering
As hunters move in, small prey escape ahead
of the flames. Wallabies, lixzards flee
their circle of heat and fear. Women collect
tubers under warm ash, wait for burnt pods
to open, store seeds in their dilly bags
for bush damper baked in slow embers.

Black boys

Potent as spears, they rise sentinel
                     after the fire has passed
New life sprouts along the blackened rod
Creamy buds crown the tip

A spray of green circles the base
Spikes wild as grass skirts
                spin as young men dance
                   Initiation stories

They learn the secrets of the Gul-gad-ya
       the power held in each spike and stem

A magic resin stronger than string
          holds spear tip to shaft
               cements an axe to the hilt

Brave Gadigal men celebrate their place
          prove their strength as hunters

make a draft from crushed flowers
their manhood stored in heady wine
              maturing with age.

Wild Honey Tour

The women take us to find honeydew, a sugar treat
rolled and licked on the fingers
tell stories of helpless slave ants kept in tunnels
large enough to fit their swelling bellies
Store pods, heavy with nectar
food for hungry workers in the dry time
We join the search for sugar ants, thump the ground
trace the hollow places
Women dance in line, sing up the tjalpa tjalpa story
with their digging sticks
collect supine honeypots, gold backs
ripe for plucking

The old men talk in language, share tribal know-how
retold by our guide
Honey-bag tales of a hive close by the waterhole
worker bees flying off
swarming on bloodwood tree, dazed by the scent
of their favourite ntewale blossoms
Small and swift they have no sting, no defence
against black hands
or lizards raiding their honey tree
Back at the hive, men find the hole, drain honey
on a stick, show us sugarbag
an easy steal, hidden inside.

Wirilda

Arrabanda women share tales of living
from the land, walking forever
through wattle country

In a good season, yellow balls blaze
with the scent of honey
Wirilda fills the desert air
Husks wait for years, for fire to open
each hard black shell, drop seeds
ripe for sprouting

I go out with the Aunties to beat
the trees with sticks, roast shiny beads
in slow embers. Pounded
to a fragrant paste, we cook
patty cakes to share warm
from a bush oven

Wirilda trees now grow on farms
to harvest the precious beans
Roasted and ground
for the bitter taste, the dark aroma
packaged as a native coffee

The bittersweet taste of wattle seed
still lingers on the tongue
Wood smoke and honey blossom
trapped inside.

Mulga stories

'That one tree, I born here,' he says.
'This my mother's place.'

We see only a scrubby bush no taller
than he, have no idea of the value
the slow growth of mulga inching year
by year, surviving dry spells

Firestick farmers caring for Country
burned patches of finger grass
to ward off lightning fires, waited
for the heat to open seed pods
buried under sand for years
Sent messages by 'mulga wire'
to warn the distant clans

He speaks fondly of this ancient tree
of many cycles yielding flowers
and seeds, a steady food always
ripe for picking. Shows us bark
easily shed for a woman's carry-all
Wood that burns brightest, cools
to a white ash good for Ceremony

Says we can call him Bill –
and he'll show us how to find flocks
of the elusive zebra finches. Up close
he spots a pair of mulga parrots
moving among the flowers
their grey green plumage soon lost
among the cover of leaves

He listens for the zip zip chip of finches
spies red beaks darting in and out
tells the story of these flashy birds
How they come each year to sip
from a juicy store of gum balls
built by the mulga wasp
thriving on Dharawala Lands

The old man looks out to a grey line
points to bare earth, dying trees
Low branches a last ditch fodder
for cattle roaming in dry seasons.

Lillipilli

At first light, I listen to sounds
on my roof, as balls drop
like the start of rain
roll down the corrugated iron
Wonder why rosellas with an eye
for colour choose the pithy flesh
send it half-ripe from the tree
Too impatient perhaps to wait
for cherries to flush red, offer
their sweet summer treat

– a nightly sugar hit
for the possum noisy in my roof
leaping at the tree with a whoosh
a baby balanced on her back

A woman arrives uninvited
at my hillside retreat. Breathless
she points to the overgrown tree
too close to my kitchen window
Gives botanical explanations
of this genus or that. Excited
by this rare example, she promises
to return, buy the ripening fruit
The perfume inside brings
a special taste, she says, to jam

I ask why rosellas peck the balls
but science has no answers
to birds who enjoy watching
me, watch their wilful play.

Larrkardiy

Ancient boabs dot the Kimberly plain
store water in their swelling trunks
for the dry time
Each part named by the ancestors
valued by Nyikina clans
for their sacred power of healing
Bush tucker to rival any health farm
or chemist's super-store

Karrakira the fruity pith, wards off colds
brings relief from pain
Ngibi seeds bring fertility to women
a strong heart to young men
making Initiation

Sharpen the sight, the wisdom
of Old Men dancing Ceremony

*

The clans no longer look for strength
from the medicine tree
settle instead for white man's tucker
bought at the Co-Op store

Kimberley farms now harvest saplings
market Larrkardiy roots
as 'specialty food'
Health and vitality guaranteed
when eaten fresh
from any suburban fridge.

dark harvest

People of the River: Derrubban

The lighthouse turns, blinks a steady eye, warns
of steep hills, unknown shores, channels moving
with the tide. No one knows how deep it is

Daylight draws in the far-off headland, as I cross
still water, drag my skiff to an inlet, deserted now
People once built stone traps, caught blackfish

feeding on sea grasses, Families would camp here
fish from bark canoes. Smoke from their fires
drifted upriver, signalled a welcome to the feast

Each narrow track leaves a trace of earlier times
records the winding journey left by generations
of Kadigul walking gently on their land

I climb high above the beach, step in footholds
cut in a rock-face, find a cave bleached by wind
and brine, a lookout shelter open to the sky

Handprints span a ledge of pristine rock, calara
scattered on the dusty floor, signal a resting place
a camp site for tribes, passing through Country

Groove-marks record skill and dexterity, across
a rock platform, flints, grinding stones lie scattered
as if discarded only yesterday by men afraid

Cries from the lookout. White clouds floating in
from the horizon, ghost strangers offering
change with gunfire along the River Country.

People of the River: Backwater

Patonga is the last stop on a road winding in
from nowhere. My headlights scan the forest
closing in, as I take the descent to a bay ringed

with lighted houses. Fishermen call over water
wait for an ebb tide, a crescent moon to set
dragnets across the bay. They trawl for prawns

massing in sandy beds, small and large caught
as they swim out to sea, the by-catch discarded
tossed to the gulls circling on the run home

Daylight draws the estuary into view as I head
up river, circle island peaks fringed with sand
Currents slow, the river branches, spreads

an arm around rows of oyster-beds. Leases
staked on tidal mudflats are failing as the city
grows closer. Acids flow in run-off after rain

threaten future life along the upper reaches
I glide to a quiet backwater where mangroves
survive steeped in brackish water. Roots breathe

capture air underwater to keep the river alive
Each year I look for young fish in the shadow
of my boat, find depleted shoals of blackfish

spawning here. They wait for a high tide
to drive them out to sea, to fishermen
setting wide nets to fill their daily quota.

Figures in a landscape

after Charles Conder, *Sydney Harbour*, 1888

1.

I watch the women from the stone veranda
as they stroll through tall grasses, place
them in the quiet space, a focal point
in a picture full of movement.

I told them not to venture far, I could see
the sky weighed down, the threat of rain
Full blown storm clouds sweep in
as I dapple a full brush across the sky.

They follow the curve of a well-worn track
downhill, parasols soon lost
under velvety figs circling the bay
in this impression of a storm breaking.

I lay down misty islands on a sea of white
quickly add a steamer heading back
to port, the harbour already washed
with grey on this monochrome day.

2.

I am not in this picture. Invisible, I fall
easily into shadow, watch the ladies walk
float white as sails on water. Ignore
the man waving from the house.

They wander, as dark clouds mass above
peer into rock pools, where we once
collected guatuma, a fishing site
of the Gadigal we still call Banarung.

I smell rain on the changing air, salt fresh
it blows in from Dharawal Land, drives
wind over water, the party soon lost
from view in the mist and spray.

Rising voices startle parrots sheltering
from the storm. The gentleman paints on
as pitching rain, claps of thunder
drown out the women's cries for help.

Monument

Captain Cook Memorial, High Cross, Randwick

He stands, marks a corner where many roads cross. Some point north, run west, fall east to the sea. Everyone has passed the stone figure on the corner, the plaque inscribed with dates to mark his presence here. This captain frowns, looks back to his ship moored in Botany Bay, one hand on his instruments. Claxton and charts mark his trade as a man of science, sent to study the movement of stars drawn across unknown oceans far from the familiar arc of the world. He maps coastlines for future exploration, records facts in terse lines, the language of discovery compressed in diary notes.

No one asks us who made the sandy tracks worn by the coming and going of bare feet. Generations of Bidjigal people walking to 'Yira-yirara', following trade routes north to the Gadigal or west to the swamplands of the Dharug. Silent, we keep watch, fade into 'wadanggari' and saltbush. Follow him when he leads his clan, strangers with firesticks, on the long climb to the highest ridge. Resting, he looks about him, the sun beating down, ignores the tracks falling away on every side. We watch as he plants the flag of conquest here, creates a new story that changes the meaning of everything that came before.

At the Falls Bundanoon I

after *Fairy Bower Rorschach*, Ben Quilty

The artist works the paint with his hands
adds great swaths of umber. Titanium
gleams under the weight of oil. Caught
in the act of falling, white water surges
from a sudden precipice. A mirror image
reflects the centrifugal energy, stirs up
a wild discourse across his tableau.
Local settlers, heard the roar, found
the track hidden among ferns. Visitors
picnic parties sought out the wonder
fancied a vital magic in the air. Fairies
were said to hide in the rainbow spray
weave charms around couples, lovers
looking for romance in reflective pools.

At the Falls Bundanoon II

He paces the floor, pushes oily pigments
towards the centre of his picture. Heavy
with black, they slip and slide, thick as
finger-paint pressed under glass. Folded
back each panel reveals old wounds
smeared across a damaged landscape.
Opens a dialogue for reinterpretation
This is no place of wonderment or renewal.
There is no magic, no sprites to leap from
the bower. Darker forces half-revealed
hide behind the weight of water. Whispers
of ancient rites surface on shallow ponds.
Below the falls, stories of desecration
and death flow on through tribal memory.

Bennelong

Dressed in the British best, he sees power
in a ruffled shirt, gains celebrity in
his time. Earns status as a go-between
Walks in both worlds, admired by all
Only his name survives to claim the Point
for the Gadigal clan, bring authenticity
to this sacred bora, famous for corroboree
Now his place bears a canopy shaped
from native gadjan, bleached by sun
and wind, found in middens across the bay
This icon billows white as the first ships
floating in to take his headland. Spirits old
and new ring a harbour speckled with light
Mask the pull of stars hidden under blackness.

Cullen Bullen

The bus takes the old road from Lithgow
past signs to Capertee, Wallerawang,
        Tarana, Ben Bullen

Places echoing tribal words, their meaning
lost, misspelt by settlers moving onto Country

I follow the road to 'Invincible Colliery', pace
the high fence, count the stakes on cyclone wire
Ignore warnings of 'Danger' and 'Keep Out'

This working mine has cut a swath for miles
worked underground 'til the last seam is spent
Up close, I find a hill sliced in two, the cliff-face
                      left gaping red

Remember fragments passed down. Generations
        of hillside burials, ground slaked
with the blood of Ancestors after 'the Round Up'

Their stories buried deep as denial

Now I read of new plans for an open-cut, posted
                by 'the Company'
With tunnels closed, the giant scrapers will scour
            remnant rock for coking coal
until the last tree and gully are stripped away

                *

Google has nothing to say about the clans
        on Cullen Bullen
              fleeing men on horses

Instead, we read of adventurers
Prospectors searching for treasure
Rivers of gold, here for the taking. Settlers
farmers taming the land with sheep

The web reports on wealthy Developers,
                    building roads over hunting tracks
Woodland cleared to mine the black rock
                    in the name of progress

Has nothing to say on our history, First People
living, thriving here, who left without a trace
Driven off Country. Lost in plain sight.

Lady Mungo

'You didn't find her. She found you.' – Mary Pappen, Mutti Mutti Elder

Knots of her spine break the shifting surface
        shape knobs of toes
              round an elbow
Knuckles cradle the small crock of her skull
        boned white by sun and wind

Painted ochres sprinkle the desert sand
        leave signs of Ceremony
a ritual farewell for a young woman
        cremated with care

She leaves a message   tells a story of her tribe
        settled on the edge of an inland sea
Reminds us of this ancient People   thinking
            looking like us
their bones no different from ours

They walked this land for millennia
        as the ice melted away
Lived well on their land flush with fish
        and waterbirds

Locked in a casket her grave no longer rests
        in sandy earth   on Country
Scientists have measured   proved her size
        her ancestry   her age
Mark her place with a memorial plinth

Wary of her removal   Tribal Elders 'smoke'
her bones   mourn her spirit left
to wander uneasy on the shifting plain.

Nukkan ya, Ruby: 'See you, Ruby'

Tribute concert to Ruby Hunter

'You're like a tree' she said   wraps
me round   arms a velvet embrace
            cool to the touch

She yields a powerful spirit   shares
her love   compassion   a joy too big
           for her tiny frame

She looks up   head thrown back
Black eyes dance   laughter springs
           into 'Koorongk'

Honey notes roll   she lifts a smile
sways her body   a slow heart
           beating her song

Sings 'I am a woman'   'Feeling Good'
We hear her story   how life   love
           'Held Up to the Moon'

She sobs her pain   her loss   asks
'Who's to Blame'   yearning to call
           her Ngarrindjeri home.

Jandamarra

adter Paul Stanhope, *The Land is Healed*
Perfomance, Sydney Opera House, 2014

High walls of sound ring the gorge once more
children whisper sacred notes in language
sing to heal their wounded land, call up
the Unggud Junba. A Great Snake returns
with sacred water to wash away the blood
the stain spreading on Bunuba Country
Brass and drums battle against their song
of suffering and regret, gunfire ricochets
Cymbals clash painted warriors against settler
Jandamarra's cry of resistance and daring
echoes through hidden caves along the creek
Young lips ripple his secret river awake
Their song shapes the hero's epic journey
fills the vault with Jalgangurru Dreaming.

Boab Tree, Derby

Step on the coach. First stop is our famous 'Prison Tree', now a 'protected site' and a great photo opportunity. On the way, listen to the voice-over, hear our pioneer story... Here we are, see the door cut in the hollow trunk. Go inside. Space for you and a few natives in that cell! Hundreds of travellers before you have cut their names deep in the bark, left their mark forever on our sunburnt country.

A fading photo on a board tells another story. Under the boab tree, initiated men line up in chains for the camera. They wear metal collars like wild dogs or wandering strays. Tribal leaders, who have never seen the sea, rounded up by 'blackbirders' on horses. 'Clevermen', keepers of Ceremony, taken off Country to break up the tribe. Kidnapped, to slave on luggers, diving for pearls off the Derby coast.

Chained together we wait in the heat. Metal collars chafe as we look up to the canopy. Remember our favourite 'larrkardiy', teaching our children to climb, harvest bush medicine to keep them strong. A lifetime of knowledge binds us to this sacred tree. We shrink from the trunk. Fear the sacred bones of ancestors, proud Nyikina men stored in the hollow. Feel the power and anger of 'Malaji' rising.

possession
wild frontier gossip
dark tourism

exploitation
tribal memory exposed
in black and white

dislocation
generations of shame
the white man's harvest

Jaga Jaga

after sand-blasted glass window panels, Nillimbuk Arts Centre, Victoria

Sharp-cut the grinder stamps his name
        from the outside looking in
A sound, a name held on the tongue
        of the Old People

Our hero's story passed down in detail
– river landings, confrontation

Skirmishes branded in Kulin memory

Words line up to chronicle the history
   trace names and dates in dry point

– knowledge etched in mission script
tell of long days sloping the pen

Forged in heat and sand, glass holds
   our truth up to the sky

hard as a window cold to the touch.

Earth hour

He is a man without a shadow
living in the park. Humid nights sleeping
behind the kiosk. Or in the undergrowth
his dark shape spread on ivy. He wakes
to the murmur of couples stumbling
on the path. Footsteps on grass
Settles to the steady roll of traffic
possums feeding on the native plums
the strange sight of a city with no light.

On 'the one night of the year' he looks
to the blacked-out city. His eyes trace
Seven Sisters Dreaming racing
across the sky. From the west to east
they pinprick the velvet canopy, create
Song cycles for his sacred places
When the sun comes up, they fall
to the sea over Bundjalung Country
leave their stories ringing in his head.

Singing the land

We go along, making country... Going there, to where the white clouds are rising. Step by step, we sing as we go, making the country. – Translation of a sacred song (Yolngu Nation)

They beat the ground with pointed sticks
    feel the thunder below
look for 'right way' tree for Ceremony
A Yidaki man taps a stringybark
    hollowed by termites
listens for the low hum
    the thrum inside
draws in a sacred Yonglu song

Barton plays new music   holds
his didjeridu with pride   calls up
    his *Kakadungu* story
I hear   thudding horses
broken lines of continuous sound
    the clash of cultures
        on cymbals and drum
Low notes resonate   each breath
  vibrates with anger and loss
carries sound patterns of the Yolngu
through concert halls across the world

Along the quay painted Kooris
play the didge   add clapsticks
chant to sell their CDs
Amplified   the music thunders
    under my feet
wakes the yidaki spirit   first music
    singing this ancient land.

Notes

dead centre

Echidna Chasm
Echidna Chasm: Bungle Bungle Purnululu National Park, West Kimberley
echidna: from Classical Greek

Dead Centre
Mithaka, Pitta Pitta: Aboriginal Nations, south-west Queensland
Kullili: Aboriginal tribe, Wangkumara Nation, Simpson Desert

Red Centre
Mparntwe: Alice Springs
Kadaji: Spirit Men (Pitjantjatjara)
Mala: Wallaby Spirit
tchurunga: Aboriginal sacred objects.

Walmadany
Walmadany: James Price Point, Western Australia
The Bay: Browse Basin
Goolarabaloo: a tribe holding native title

Kumerang
Kumerang: Hindmarsh Island
Doreen Kartinyeri: chief litigant in the Hindmarsh Island Court Case
Yarraldi: Hindmarsh Island clan
Ngarrendjeri: Aboriginal Nation, south-east South Australia

Poor fella Country
dream-up: 'sing' the Dreaming
Sacred Caterpillar: Arrernte Dreaming story
On Country: Aboriginal land

Piccaninny Gorge
Piccaninny Gorge: the Bungle Bungle
Purnululu National Park, Northern Territory
Ngarranggarni: west Kimberley Country
Gidgi and Djaru: Aboriginal Language groups

right season

Bush Tucker Tour
witjuri: witchetty grub
tnyeme: wattle bush (Arrernte language)

Mingulpa
mingkulpa: native 'tobacco' plant (Pitjinjarra)
tjulpa: white alkaline ash
a quid: small plug

Black boys
gulgadya: black boys or grass trees
Gadigal: Port Jackson Aboriginal tribe

Wild Honey Tour
honeybag, sugarbag: wild honey
ntewale: bloodwood flower
Tjalpa Tjalpa: Honey-ant Dreaming (Arrernte)

Wirilda
wirilda: desert wattle
Kokartha: Aboriginal Nation, South Australia
bush tucker food: bush food industry

Mulga stories
mulga: acacia aneura
mulga wire: smoke signals
Dharawala: Aboriginal Nation, south-west Queensland

dark harvest

People of the River: Deerubban
Deerubban: Hawkesbury River
Guringal: Guringai clans: the River People
garuma: blackfish
calara: large river mussel
River Country: Brisbane Waters National Park

Figures in a Landscape
guatuma: Sydney rock oysters
Gadigal: the Sydney tribe
Banarung: Rose Bay
Dharawal Land: the Illawarra

Monument
Bidjigal: Botany Bay tribe
Yirra-yirara: Sydney Cove
Dharug: Western Sydney tribe
wadanggari: coastal banksia

Bennelong
Gadigal clan: local group, Sydney
bora: circle cleared for Ceremony

Lady Mungo
tribal elders: from Paakantji, Ngiampaa and Mutti Mutti People

Nukkan ya, Ruby: 'See you, Ruby'
Ngarrindjeri: Aboriginal Nation, lower Murray River

Jandamarra
'The Land is Healed', by Paul Stanhope, text by Steve Hawke, sung in Bunura language, performed at the Sydney Opera House, July 2014, Yilimbirri Ensemble, Gondwana Children's Choir and Chorale with the Sydney Symphony Orchestra

Boab Tree Derby
larrkardiy: the boab or medicine tree (Ngarrangkani)
Malaji: spirit, protector of the Nyikina tribe
the Kimberley, Western Australia

Jaga Jaga
Kulin: Aboriginal Nation, south central Victoria

Earth hour
Bundjalung Country: north coast NSW
Seven Sisters Dreaming: Aboriginal song cycle (The Pleiades)

Singing the land
yidaki: traditional instrument
'Kalkadungu': music for voice, didjeridu, electric guitar and orchestra by Mathew Hinson and William Barton, Kalkadungu tribe, Queensland

www.ingramcontent.com/pod-product-compliance
Lightning Source LLC
Chambersburg PA
CBHW062146100526
44589CB00014B/1698